PAMPHLETS ON AMERICAN WRITERS · NUMBER 8

UNIVERSITY OF MINNESOTA

T. S. Eliot

BY LEONARD UNGER

UNIVERSITY OF MINNESOTA PRESS · MINNEAPOLIS

Printed in the United States of America at the
Lund Press, Inc., Minneapolis

Library of Congress Catalog Card Number: 61-62512

third printing 1967

PUBLISHED IN GREAT BRITAIN, INDIA, AND PAKISTAN BY THE OXFORD UNIVERSITY
PRESS, LONDON, BOMBAY, AND KARACHI, AND IN CANADA BY THE COPP
CLARK PUBLISHING CO. LIMITED, TORONTO

T. S. ELIOT

Leonard Unger is a professor of English at the University of Minnesota. He is the editor of *T. S. Eliot: A Selected Critique* and the author of *The Man in the Name: Essays on the Experience of Poetry*.

⤲ *T. S. Eliot*

I PERCEIVED that I myself had always been a New Englander in the South West [meaning St. Louis, Missouri], and a
South Westerner in New England." This comment of T. S. Eliot's,
referring to his childhood and youth in the United States, was
published in 1928 — a year after he had become an English subject
and had entered the Church of England. About thirty years later,
in an interview conducted in New York, he affirmed that his poetry
belongs in the tradition of American literature: "I'd say that my
poetry has obviously more in common with my distinguished con-
temporaries in America, than with anything written in my generation in England. That I'm sure of." To the question whether there
was "a connection with the American past," he answered: "Yes,
but I couldn't put it any more definitely than that, you see. It
wouldn't be what it is, and I imagine it wouldn't be so good; put-
ting it as modestly as I can, it wouldn't be what it is if I'd been
born in England, and it wouldn't be what it is if I'd stayed in
America. It's a combination of things. But in its sources, in its emo-
tional springs, it comes from America." (The interview from which
this and other statements are quoted was conducted by Mr. Donald
Hall, and appears in the *Paris Review*, Number 21, Spring–Summer
1959.)

The poet's parents were both descended from old New England
families. His paternal grandfather had come to St. Louis from
Harvard Divinity School to establish the city's first Unitarian
church and then to found and preside over Washington University. His father, Henry Ware Eliot, became president of a local
industry, the Hydraulic Press Brick Company of St. Louis. His

mother, Charlotte Chauncey Stearns, is the author of a long poem on the life of Savonarola and an extended biography of her father-in-law. Thomas Stearns Eliot, the youngest of seven children, was born September 26, 1888. In his own words, the family in St. Louis "guarded jealously its connexions with New England."

After attending the Smith Academy in St. Louis, Eliot completed his preparation for college at the Milton Academy in Massachusetts and then entered Harvard in the fall of 1906, where he pursued philosophy as his major field of study. As an undergraduate he edited and contributed poems to the *Harvard Advocate*. He completed the college course in three years and then continued to study philosophy in the Graduate School, with an interruption for one year's study (1910–11) at the Sorbonne. In 1914 he returned to Europe, studying first in Germany and then, after the outbreak of the war, at Oxford. Although he completed a doctoral dissertation on the philosophy of F. H. Bradley, he never returned to Harvard for formal acceptance of the degree. After marrying Vivienne Haigh Haigh-Wood in 1915, Eliot was employed briefly as a teacher of various subjects at a boy's school near London, and after that at Lloyds Bank. A physical condition prevented him from entering the U.S. Navy in 1918. From 1917 to 1919 he was assistant editor of the *Egoist*, and for that period and the years immediately following, besides writing poetry, he supported himself by writing for magazines and periodicals reviews and essays, some of which have since become famous. Eliot's personal literary relations led him into the publishing business — eventually to become a director of Faber and Faber, a position which he still holds. He became editor of the *Criterion* at its outset in 1922, a quarterly review which played an important part in literary developments for the period of its duration. (It ceased publication, by Eliot's decision, at the approach of World War II.) After an absence of eighteen years, he returned to the United States in order to give the Charles Eliot Norton lectures at Harvard in 1932–33. He has since made frequent visits to his native country, lecturing and giving readings at various institutions, and accepting official awards of honor. The British Order of Merit and the Nobel Prize for Literature were awarded to him in 1948, and other distinctions of international eminence have followed. In 1947 his first wife died, after prolonged illness and residence in a nursing home. In January of 1957 Eliot married Miss Valerie Fletcher, who had been his private secretary.

It would be too crudely simple to regard the divided regional identity of Eliot's youth as the cause of qualities which have characterized his thought and work. But this early dual identity does prefigure and illustrate a large and inclusive pattern. Eliot was both Westerner and New Englander, but not wholly one or the other. So with his migration to England and Englishness. In his early literary criticism, the prose of the twenties and thirties, there are sometimes tones and gestures which out-English the English as only a foreigner, and perhaps only an American, could do. In religion he became a "Catholic" and an apologist for Catholicism, but he is not a Roman Catholic. His criticism urged a program of the classical, the traditional, and the impersonal, while he was producing a poetry which is poignantly romantic, strikingly modernist, and intensely personal. When others protested that there was a marked contradiction between his theory and his practice, Eliot explained: "In one's prose reflexions one may be legitimately occupied with ideals, whereas in the writing of verse one can only deal with actuality." And yet, in the later stages of his career Eliot has frequently referred to the intimate relation between his prose — especially the discussions of specific poets — and his own poetry. Of that kind of criticism — which he has called "workshop criticism" — he has said that it has been an attempt "to defend the kind of poetry he is writing, or to formulate the kind he wants to write," and again, that "its merits and its limitations can be fully appreciated only when it is considered in relation to the poetry I have written myself."

Eliot's boyhood enthusiasms for poetry were commonplace enough, and yet they also prefigure his own development. At the age of fourteen he was deeply impressed and excited by the *Rubaiyat*, and then by Byron and Swinburne — for all the differences, a body of poetry marked by melancholy, cynicism, and cleverness. But it was at about the age of nineteen, while he was a junior at Harvard University, that an event took place which was to be of the greatest importance to Eliot as a poet — and to the course of English poetry in the twentieth century. The event was his discovery of *The Symbolist Movement in Literature*, a book on the French symbolist writers of the nineteenth century by the English critic Arthur Symons. Eliot was eventually to be influenced, in a general way, by several of the French poets, from Baudelaire to Mallarmé, but it was Jules Laforgue, discovered through Symons' book, who was to have by far the greatest effect. Eliot's acknowledgment of this is well known: "The form in which I began to write, in 1908 or 1909, was directly drawn from the study of Laforgue together with the later Elizabethan drama; and I do not know anyone who started from exactly that point." Insofar as Eliot started from an *exact point*, it was exclusively and emphatically the poetry of Laforgue. The later Elizabethan dramatists had a less immediate and less intense effect, and their influence is not positively apparent until "Gerontion," which was written about ten years after the initial encounter with Laforgue. The early poems published in the *Harvard Advocate* during 1909–10 read like translations or adaptations from Laforgue. "Conversation Galante," included in *Prufrock and Other Observations*, still has a highly imitative quality and serves very well to illustrate the first stages of influence. The poem is obviously modeled on "Autre

8

Complainte de Lord Pierrot," which is quoted entire by Symons. These two stanzas are enough to show the closeness between the two poems:

> Et si ce cri lui part: "Dieu de Dieu que je t'aime!"
> — "Dieu reconnaîtra les siens." Ou piquée au vif:
> — "Mes claviers ont du cœur, tu sera mon seul thème."
> Moi: "Tout est relatif."

✦ ✦ ✦

> And I then: "Someone frames upon the keys
> That exquisite nocturne, with which we explain
> The night and moonshine; music which we seize
> To body forth our own vacuity."
> She then: "Does this refer to me?"
> "Oh no, it is I who am inane."

If we consider these two poems, Laforgue's and Eliot's, and then recall Eliot's "Portrait of a Lady," it is easy to see how that poem, too, is another *conversation galante*, a dialogue between a man and a woman in which at once too much and too little is being communicated. In like manner, the *Harvard Advocate* poem called "Spleen" may be seen as a rudimentary form of "The Love Song of J. Alfred Prufrock." This early poem records the distraction and dejection produced by the "procession . . . of Sunday faces," by the social routines of the day and the sordid aspects of an urban alley, and then ends with a personification of "Life" as a balding and graying man, fastidiously attired and mannered, waiting with self-conscious correctness as a social caller upon the "Absolute." But "Prufrock" is also related to the "Portrait" and "Conversation Galante." The poem opens with the promise "To lead you to an overwhelming question . . ." and this question is not so much an interrogation as a problem — the problem of communication between a man and a woman.

> And would it have been worth it, after all,
> After the cups, the marmalade, the tea . . .

> To have squeezed the universe into a ball
> To roll it toward some overwhelming question,
> To say: "I am Lazarus, come from the dead,
> Come back to tell you all, I shall tell you all" —
> If one, settling a pillow by her head
>> Should say: "That is not what I meant at all.
>> That is not it, at all."

This theme of the failure of communication, of a positive relationship, between a man and a woman is found again in the other early poems "Hysteria" and "La Figlia che Piange," and it is indeed a major theme of the whole body of Eliot's work. It appears early in *The Waste Land* with the image of the "hyacinth girl."

> — Yet when we came back, late, from the Hyacinth garden,
> Your arms full, and your hair wet, I could not
> Speak, and my eyes failed, I was neither
> Living nor dead, and I knew nothing,
> Looking into the heart of light, the silence.

This theme is developed by various means throughout Eliot's poetry and plays. It becomes related to other emerging themes, especially to religious meanings — for example, in the symbolic imagery of the "rose-garden" which appears in *Ash Wednesday*, *Four Quartets*, *The Family Reunion*, and *The Confidential Clerk*.

One of the most familiar aspects of Eliot's poetry is its complex echoing of multiple sources. In the early poems, those of the "Prufrock" period, this aspect is not yet very marked, but it is nonetheless already present in some degree. The title "Portrait of a Lady" immediately suggests Henry James, and there is indeed much about this poetry which is Jamesian. For one thing, the theme of the man-woman relationship frustrated or imperfectly realized is a common one in James's fiction. Commentators have noticed particularly a similarity of situations in Eliot's poem and the short novel called *The Beast in the Jungle* — in which the protagonist becomes poignantly and devastatingly aware of a woman's love for him only after she had died. Besides this specific similarity, there is a general Jamesian atmosphere which pervades the early poems. The man and woman of the "Portrait," Prufrock himself, "The readers of the *Boston Evening Transcript*," Aunt Helen, Cousin Nancy, the foreign Mr. Apollinax and his American hosts, all are Jamesian personae. Eliot, like James, presents a world of genteel society, as it is seen from within, but seen also with critical penetration, with a consciousness that is deliberately and intensely self-consciousness. Both writers, in their ultimate meanings, show a liberation from the genteel standard of decorum, while the style and manner which have familiarly attended the decorum not only remain, but have become more complicated and intense. After the period of the early poems, the Jamesian qualities, like the Laforguean, are not abandoned but are assimilated and survive in the later stages of development. The opening strophe of *The Waste Land*, with its vision of a cosmopolitan society, ends on a Jamesian note: "I read, much of the night, and go south in the winter." The Jamesian quality emerges with great clarity in all the plays on contemporary subjects. They are all set in James-like genteel worlds. Such dramatic intensity as they have resides, as in so much of James's fiction, in crises of sensibility and awareness. Significantly enough, a specific Jamesian note is strongly sounded at the opening of the earliest of these plays. In the very first minute of *The Family Reunion* Ivy echoes *The Waste Land* with rather heavy emphasis:

> I have always told Amy she should go south in the winter.
> Were I in Amy's position, I would go south in the winter. . . .
> I would go south in the winter, if I could afford it . . .

In the same scene, only a few minutes later, Agatha is commenting on Harry's return to his parental home, and she speaks the phrase "it will not be a very *jolly* corner," thus invoking Henry James, who had written a story called "The Jolly Corner," also about a man's homecoming and his search for an earlier identity.

While the theme of estrangement between man and woman is, so to speak, an ultimate subject throughout much of Eliot's work, it also signifies the larger theme of the individual's isolation, his estrangement from other people and from the world. There are intimations of this larger theme even in "Portrait of a Lady," where the young man's twice mentioned "self-possession" means not only his *poise* but, in the Eliotic context, his isolation, his inability to give himself to or to possess others. In "Prufrock" the theme of isolation is pervasive and represented in various ways, from the "patient etherised upon a table," at the beginning, to the mermaids, at the end, who will not "sing to me" — but especially in the well-known lines

> I should have been a pair of ragged claws
> Scuttling across the floors of silent seas.

In a sense, all of Eliot's works in verse are variations on the theme of isolation. *The Waste Land* presents a procession of characters locked within themselves. The subject emerges into definition toward the end of the poem.

> We think of the key, each in his prison
> Thinking of the key, each confirms a prison . . .

When we turn to the plays, we find characters either accepting isolation or struggling to escape from it. In *Murder in the Cathedral*, the saint, Thomas, is by definition set apart from ordinary humanity. Harry, toward the end of *The Family Reunion*, says, "Where does one go from a world of insanity?" — and the implication of his subsequent and final statement is that he goes the way of the saint and the martyr. This is the way, too, that Celia Coplestone goes in *The Cocktail Party*, while the estranged Edward and Lavinia Chamberlayne are reconciled, not to love, or even to understanding, but merely to mutual toleration, making "the best of a bad job." The theme of isolation is in focus throughout the play, and with especial clarity in such words as these of Celia to the psychiatrist, Sir Henry Harcourt-Reilly:

> No . . . it isn't that I *want* to be alone,
> But that everyone's alone — or so it seems to me.
> They make noises, and think that they are talking
>   to each other;
> They make faces, and think they understand each other.
> And I'm sure that they don't.

Unlike the earlier plays, *The Confidential Clerk* contains no suggestion of the martyred saint, but nonetheless the central character, Colby Simpkins, like Harry and Celia before him, goes his own way. Finally indifferent as to who are his earthly parents, he turns to religion, first to be a church organist, and probably in time an Anglican clergyman. *The Cocktail Party* and *The Confidential Clerk* are each in turn, and with increasing measure, departures from the extreme and intense isolation represented in *The Family Reunion*. In *The Cocktail Party* marriage is regarded as a way of life, though cheerless, yet necessary and acceptable, "the common routine." *The Confidential Clerk* offers a brighter perspective on marriage and on the possibilities of mutual sympathy and understanding among human beings.

Then, with *The Elder Statesman*, there is the most marked departure of all from the theme of isolation. Lord Claverton, invalided and retired statesman and business executive of hollow success, has been a failure as friend, lover, husband, and father. His frustrations and anxieties are dramatized by the return of the man and woman whom in his youth he had abused. But his daughter Monica and her fiancé Charles encourage him to explain his problems, and in explaining he confesses all the pretenses and deceptions of his life, while they listen with an understanding and sympathy which restore him to himself and thus release him from his isolation. He discovers not only the love which Monica and Charles have for him, but also the love which they have for each other. In *The Elder Statesman*, Eliot has for the first time depicted with ardency and exaltation real and normal relations between a man and a woman. Toward the very end of the play, Charles tells Monica that he loves her "to the limits of speech, and beyond." And she replies that she has loved him "from the beginning of the world," that this love which has brought them together "was always there," before either of them was born. As compared to Eliot's other plays, there is no apparent religious dimension in *The Elder Statesman* — except for the intimations of these words of Monica. The play is an affirmation of human relations, a drama of escape from isolation within the limits of those relations.

It has been said of some writers that they write as if no one has ever written before. Of Eliot it is the reverse which is true — and true with a special significance, so that one cannot speak of his *sources* in the usual scholarly fashion. The point is that Eliot has been in a respect his own scholar, having brought to his work not only the influence of his sources but what might more aptly be called an awareness of his predecessors. This is true in a variety of ways. For example, the theme of isolation is so obviously universal and so readily available that a writer might very well pursue it without any awareness of particular antecedents or analogues. But for Eliot there is such an awareness. This is indicated by the footnote which Eliot fixed to the "key-prison" passage of *The Waste Land*. The footnote refers us to *Appearance and Reality*, a work by the British philosopher F. H. Bradley, and quotes as follows from that work: "My external sensations are no less private to myself than are my thoughts or my feelings. In either case my experience falls within my own circle, a circle closed on the outside; and, with all its elements alike, every sphere is opaque to the others which surround it. . . . In brief, regarded as an existence which appears in a soul, the whole world for each is peculiar and private to that soul." Eliot's deep interest in this idealist philosopher is indicated by his unpublished Harvard doctoral thesis (1916), "Experience and the Objects of Knowledge in the Philosophy of F. H. Bradley," and by a few other pieces, one of which is included in his *Selected Essays*. The Bradleyan element in Eliot's thought emerges as an echo of the circle image in one of the choruses of *The Family Reunion*.

> But the circle of our understanding
> Is a very restricted area.
> Except for a limited number
> Of strictly practical purposes
> We do not know what we are doing;
> And even, when you think of it,
> We do not know much about thinking.
> What is happening outside the circle?
> And what is the meaning of happening?

To consider further the relationship between source and theme in Eliot, we can return to the writings of Jules Laforgue and to the chapter on him in Arthur Symons' book. Laforgue had written a number of prose tales which he called collectively *Moralités Légendaires*. Among the stories which Laforgue retold with witty and ironical modernization, there is one called "Hamlet"; and in his chapter Symons quotes, using his own translation, a passage from Laforgue's version of the graveyard monologue, part of which follows: "Ah! I would like to set out to-morrow, and search all through the world for the most adamantine processes of embalming. They, too, were, the little people of History, learning to read, trimming their nails, lighting the dirty lamp every evening, in love, gluttonous, vain, fond of compliments, hand-shakes, and kisses, living on bell-tower gossip, saying, 'What sort of weather shall we have to-morrow? Winter has really come. . . . We have had no plums this year.'"

Aside from the question of possible echoes in Eliot's work, one may find in this passage a quality of voice, of rhythm and tone, which is also a quality of Eliot's poetry, from "Prufrock" to *The Elder Statesman*. One way of testing the similarity, if it is not immediately obvious, would be to recite any section of "Preludes" and then turn to Laforgue — "They, too, were," etc. — and continue *reciting*. As for specific echoing, it comes at a point in Eliot's development when, according to several critics, the Laforguean influence was supposed to have been left far behind. In the second Chorus of *Murder in the Cathedral* the Women of Canterbury describe themselves as *les petites gens de l'Histoire* — in their own words, as "the small folk drawn into the pattern of fate, the small folk who live among small things." And these "small folk," like the *petites gens*, speak of weather, seasons, and the failure of the plums:

> Sometimes the corn has failed us,
> Sometimes the harvest is good,
> One year is a year of rain,
> Another a year of dryness,
> One year the apples are abundant,
> Another year the plums are lacking.
> Yet we have gone on living,
> Living and partly living.

Returning to the question of theme, we recall readily that Shakespeare's character Hamlet has been during and since the nineteenth century the symbol par excellence of isolation and alienation. Laforgue's modernization of the character has significantly the quality of parody, for in his Hamlet self-consciousness has been intensified to the point of self-irony and self-mockery, to the emphatically non-heroic — the seed of which already exists in Shakespeare's play. Prufrock is himself already a Laforguean Hamlet, an early Eliotic Hamlet, in making the analogy by negation: "No! I am not Prince Hamlet, nor was meant to be." But neither is Prufrock one of the "lonely men in shirt-sleeves, leaning out of windows." The "men in shirt-sleeves" residing in "narrow streets" are typical figures in that modern landscape, comprising both human and nonhuman elements, which stretches through so much of Eliot's work. And it is a landscape which is continuous with the vision Laforgue's Hamlet has of people "trimming their nails, lighting the dirty lamp every evening, in love, gluttonous, vain," etc. Eliot has defined his position by vividly portraying the world from which he is isolated and alienated. This practice is consistent with the Bradleyan philosophy. The individual mood, the quality of consciousness, the private feeling, is continuous with, in a sense identical with, the seemingly objective material that has provoked it. A person's identity is defined by his world, and to escape one is as difficult as to escape the other. This concept is implied in that early poem "Spleen," where a "waste land" is already beginning to emerge, where an environment of people and things is a "dull conspiracy" against which depression is "unable to rally." Prufrock's escape to the beautiful and the ideal from the ugly and the real, his reverie of the mermaids, is only momentarily sustained, "Till human voices wake us, and we drown."

Characteristically, the moments of beauty in Eliot's work are meagre and brief and are obviously calculated to serve as a contrasting emphasis on the opposite, as in *The Waste Land*:

> the nightingale
> Filled all the desert with inviolable voice
> And still she cried, and still the world pursues,
> "Jug Jug" to dirty ears.

Up through *The Waste Land* Eliot's poetry is richly furnished with images of the sordid, the disgusting, and the depressing, and with personalities of similar quality. In the poems of the "Prufrock" group (1917) there are the one-night cheap hotels and sawdust restaurants, the vacant lots, faint stale smells of beer, a thousand furnished rooms and the yellow soles of feet, the dead geraniums, the broken spring in a factory yard, all the old nocturnal smells, the basement kitchens, and the damp souls of housemaids. In the poems of the "Gerontion" group (1920), there are "Rocks, moss, stonecrop, iron, merds," and such obnoxious persons as Bleistein, Sweeney, and Grishkin. *The Waste Land* (1922) and *The Hollow Men* (1925) are titles indicating clearly enough the grounds of alienation. *The Waste Land* is a grand consummation of the themes, techniques, and styles that Eliot had been developing, and *The Hollow Men* is at once an epilogue to that development and a prologue to a new stage in the career.

The new stage is marked by the difference between the titles *The Hollow Men* and *Ash Wednesday*, and by Eliot's entry into the Church of England in 1927. But the new stage is not, of course, a sudden and abrupt change. Its emergence may be seen, especially in retrospect, in the prose — even as early as 1917, the date of "Tradition and the Individual Talent," which is relevant both by its title and its general argument — and the emergence may be seen in the poetry as well. The continuity of Eliot's poetry is, indeed, most impressive, already indicated here in some measure, and will be further considered. For the moment, it is appropriate to observe that *The Waste Land* and *The Hollow Men* have in retrospect been considered more Christian than they originally appeared to be. The way in which theme and imagery of *The Waste Land* blend and merge into those of *Ash Wednesday* is illustrated by these passages from *The Hollow Men*:

> This is the dead land
> This is cactus land
> Here the stone images
> Are raised, here they receive
> The supplication of a dead man's hand
> Under the twinkle of a fading star.

*   *   *

> Sightless, unless
> The eyes reappear
> As the perpetual star
> Multifoliate rose
> Of death's twilight kingdom
> The hope only
> Of empty men.

The rocks that are red in *The Waste Land* reappear in *Ash Wednesday* as cool and blue. In the one poem there is the lament "Amongst the rocks one cannot stop or think," while the other poem moves toward conclusion with the prayer

> Teach us to care and not to care
> Teach us to sit still
> Even among these rocks.

Eliot's deliberate echoing of the earlier poem in the later one signifies that the difference in position is produced by a development rather than a departure or a break. While the position of isolation and alienation from the world is the foremost theme of the poetry up through *The Waste Land*, the same position, but with respect to God, is the theme of *Ash Wednesday*. Thus the first position, considered as a problem, has not been resolved. It has, rather, been incorporated into the second position and thus reinterpreted and re-evaluated. If one does not love the world, one is already well prepared for making an effort to love God. Isolation and alienation from the world become a stage in the discipline of religious purgation, an ideal to be further pursued. With Eliot's profession of Christian belief, this is the meaning which has been found in the lines concluding *The Waste Land*:

> Shall I at least set my lands in order?
> London Bridge is falling down falling down
>   falling down
> *Poi s'ascose nel foco che gli affina* . . .

A distinction can be made between the sources and the influences which lie behind Eliot's work. Many writers have been incidental sources without having been actual influences — while all influences are, in varying ways, also sources. Laforgue was, of course, both. And so, too, was the fiction of Joseph Conrad, especially the well-known story "Heart of Darkness." As in other cases, Eliot has provided cues to the relation between himself and Conrad. The original, but deleted, epigraph to *The Waste Land* was Kurtz's whispered cry "The horror! the horror!" and then another phrase, "Mr. Kurtz — he dead," was used as epigraph to *The Hollow Men*. In *The Waste Land* there are verbal echoes of several of Conrad's works, such as the allusion to Conrad's title in the phrase "heart of light," which occurs still again in *Burnt Norton*. Such details are evidence of Eliot's use of Conrad as a source, and they may also be cues to that larger and more complex relation which is called influence, when and if it exists. The following passages from "Heart of Darkness," from Marlowe's comments on his experience after Kurtz's death and on his own return to the European city, may indicate some of the facets of the larger and more complex relation.

"I have wrestled with death. It is the most unexciting contest you can imagine. It takes place in an impalpable grayness, with nothing underfoot, with nothing around, without spectators, without clamour, without glory, without the great desire of victory, without the great fear of defeat, in a sickly atmosphere of tepid scepticism, without much belief in your own right, and still less in that of your adversary. . . .

"No, they did not bury me, though there is a period of time which I remember mistily, with a shuddering wonder, like a passage through some inconceivable world that had no hope in it and no desire. I found myself back in the sepulchral city resenting the sight of people hurrying through the streets to filch a little money from each other, to devour their infamous cookery, to gulp their unwholesome beer, to dream their insignificant and silly dreams. They trespassed upon my thoughts. They were intruders whose knowledge of life was to me an irritating pretence, because I felt so sure they could not possibly know the things I knew."

It takes only a slight effort of the "auditory imagination" to hear in these cadences of Conrad's prose the familiar rhythm and music, the voice, of Eliot's poetry. The remarkable thing is that while there are no specific and immediately recognizable borrowings by Eliot from these passages of Conrad's prose, they provoke associations along the whole range of Eliot's verse, from "Prufrock" and "Preludes" to *Four Quartets* and the plays. The effect is produced not only by the recurring rhythms of the grammatical elements, but by the combination of these with images and meanings: the distressed sensibility, the individual's isolation, the distasteful view of the external world, and the alienation from others — "they could not possibly know the things I knew." There is thus a striking similarity of tone and meaning between the passages of prose quoted here from Laforgue and Conrad. The curious fact is that we do not feel Eliot's style to be Laforguean or Conradian, but feel rather that in these passages the older writers are strangely Eliotic. Eliot has so clearly and firmly created and sustained his own style that it is his quality which we feel when we encounter some of the sources from which it derives. Because Eliot has repeated the accents of Laforgue and Conrad for his own controlled purposes, we discover that he has left something of his own accent on their language — he has tuned our ears to hear them in a special way. To hear Conrad in this way helps us understand what Eliot meant when he said (in "Swinburne as Poet," 1920) that "the language which is more important to us is that which is struggling to digest and express new objects, new groups of objects, new feelings, new aspects, as, for instance, the prose of Mr. James Joyce or the earlier Conrad."

The idea of isolation, of the impossibility of communication and understanding, has a direct bearing on Eliot's style, his mode of composition, and the structure of his poems, for the thematic problem is not only that of communication between one person and another but, finally, that of articulation itself. Prufrock, toward the end of his monologue, declares,

> It is impossible to say just what I mean!
> But as if a magic lantern threw the nerves in
> patterns on a screen . . .

This statement has a multiplicity of implications which are appropriate to Eliot's work, both the poetry and the criticism. The statement is Prufrock's, and it is also Eliot's, spoken through the mask of Prufrock. We may consider first its relevance to the poem in which it occurs. A familiar complaint about Eliot's early poetry, including "Prufrock," was that it was difficult, obscure, and so on — that it did not clearly and directly say what it means. And indeed, it does not. Instead, like the magic lantern, it throws "the nerves in patterns on a screen." The poem "Prufrock" is like a series of slides. Each slide is an isolated, fragmentary image, producing its own effect, including suggestions of some larger action or situation of which it is but an arrested moment. For example, "Prufrock" proceeds from the half-deserted streets at evening, to the women coming and going, to the yellow fog, to Prufrock descending the stair, and so on, to the mermaids at the end of the poem. Each part of the poem, each fragment, remains fragmentary even within its given context — a series of larger wholes is suggested, and yet the series of suggestions is itself a kind of whole. It is the poem. It is Prufrock. He has gone nowhere and done nothing. He has conducted an "interior monologue," as the critics have said, and he is the monologue. All the scenery of the poem, indoor and outdoor, is finally the psychological landscape of Prufrock himself. The streets, rooms, people, and fancies of the poem all register on Prufrock's consciousness, and thus they are his consciousness, the man himself. Prufrock the man, his self-awareness, his state of feeling — each is equal to the other, and to his *meaning*. In order to say *just what* he means, he must render the essential man himself, he must throw, as it were ("But as if"), the nerves in patterns on a screen. But so to project the *real* nerves, the feelings in all their fullness which are the man himself, is impossible. It is the incommunicable secret of the mystics, and the ideal of romantic lovers. It is also the myth of romantic poets, from Byron and Shelley to Whitman, and since then. And it is distinctive of Eliot's modernness, of his modern romanticism, that he knows that it is a myth, while still recognizing the impulse (which is not the same as the desire) to pursue it.

Emerging from these considerations of "Prufrock" are generalizations which are applicable to all of Eliot's poetry. The characteristic poem, whether "Prufrock" or other, is analogous to the series of slides, highly selective and suggestive. And like "Prufrock," the poem contains a statement acknowledging this aspect of the poem and of its structure. (In this regard Eliot is more conservative than the French Symbolist poets who served him as model and authority for this mode of composition.) "Preludes" is a series of four sketches of urban scenes in winter, followed by an explicatory comment:

> I am moved by fancies that are curled
> Around these images, and cling:
> The notion of some infinitely gentle
> Infinitely suffering thing.

"These images" constitute the main body of the poem. The poet has tried to guide the reader toward the "meaning" of the poem by mentioning the "fancies" which attend the images, and then by illustrating with a particular "notion." There are still other fancies or notions in the conclusion to the poem.

> Wipe your hands across your mouth, and laugh;

23

> The worlds revolve like ancient women
> Gathering fuel in vacant lots.

The final image picks up thematically from the first scene the image of "newspapers from vacant lots." The poem thus ends on the note of the fragmentary, which is in various senses the subject of the poem.

In the earlier stages of Eliot's development "Prufrock," "Gerontion," and *The Waste Land* are obviously the major landmarks. Each of these poems in turn deepens, expands, and complicates features of the preceding poem, and among such features are the theme of alienation, the fragmentary quality of the parts, and finally the acknowledgment of these within the poem. While Prufrock exclaims that it is impossible to say just what he means, Gerontion announces that he has lost all the faculties of perception:

> I have lost my sight, smell, hearing, taste and touch:
> How should I use them for your closer contact?

And Gerontion concludes with a statement which is a characterization of the monologue he has delivered:

> Tenants of the house,
> Thoughts of a dry brain in a dry season.

At the opening of the poem he calls himself "A dull head among windy spaces," and thus at the opening and close of the poem there are justifications, and hence admissions, of the nature of the poem — of its lack of conventional continuity and coherence. It is the critics who have described "Prufrock" as an "interior monologue," but it was Eliot himself who indicated the peculiarly private relevance of "Gerontion": "Thoughts of a dry brain."

As for *The Waste Land*, only a few reminders serve well to evoke the central themes and general qualities of that work. "A heap of broken images"; "I could not / Speak"; "Is there nothing in your head?"; "I can connect / Nothing with nothing"; "We think of the key, each in his prison." And then finally, at the end of the poem, among the collection of quoted fragments, there is the statement, "These fragments I have shored against my ruins." The fragments are, of course, the amalgam of quotations in which the statement is imbedded. But the statement may also be taken as a reference to the entire poem, for the whole of *The Waste Land* is in a respect an amalgam of quotations, of fragments. At the opening there are the snatches of conversation, and then the poem is under way, with the addition of fragment to fragment, selected parts of a variety of sources mingled together and flowing into each other, the sources being life itself past and present as well as writings, until all the broken images are assembled into the heap which is the poem itself, the completed mixture of memory and desire. The series of fragments at the end compresses and intensifies the technique, the mode of expression, which has operated throughout the poem. In this respect, the very technique of the poem, especially as symbolized by the conclusion, is significant of the poet's meaning — or of part of his meaning — which is his despair of ever succeeding in fully articulating his meaning. If the poet's own voice finally fails him, he can at least intimate that much, confirm his prison, by withdrawing almost altogether, while the poem dies away with the echo of other voices, and thus reaches a termination which is, appropriately, not altogether a conclusion. It is impossible for the poet to say *just* what he means, and yet he manages to say that much. And to say that much, to say it effectively, to make the claim persuasively, is after all a kind of consummation. If he could have entirely articulated his meaning, then it would no longer have been the meaning with which he was concerned.

There are external facts related to these subjects of the fragmentary and the problem of articulation. It is well known, for example, that the form in which *The Waste Land* was published was the result of Ezra Pound's extensive editing of Eliot's manuscript.

We do not know precisely and fully what changes Pound made, for the original manuscript seems to be irretrievably lost. But we know quite a bit, from surviving correspondence between Pound and Eliot and from Eliot's testimony. Pound persuaded Eliot not to use as epigraph a quotation from Conrad's "Heart of Darkness," not to use "Gerontion" as a prelude to *The Waste Land*, to retain the section called "Death by Water" (which is Eliot's translation of his own French verses in "Dans le Restaurant"), and to accept excisions which reduced the poem to about half its original length. Eliot's decision to accept Pound's recommendations is, of course, part of his own creative responsibility and achievement, but it also forcibly illustrates the essential fragmentariness of Eliot's work. *The Waste Land* could survive, and with benefit, the amputation of fragments because it was and is essentially an arrangement of fragments. But it is no more so than the poetry that had been written earlier and the poetry that was to follow. Both *The Hollow Men* and *Ash Wednesday* (published in 1925 and 1930 respectively) began as short individual poems published independently in periodicals, and the pieces were later fitted together and other sections added to make the completed longer poems. This piecemeal mode of composition is emphasized by the fact that some of the short poems written during the same period and having similar themes, style, and imagery are excluded from *The Hollow Men* and in the collected editions preserved among the "Minor Poems." There is a nice implication here — that "minor" pieces, when assembled under an inclusive title and according to some thematic and cumulative principle, produce a "major" and more formidable whole. The relationship between whole and parts is again suggested by the "Ariel Poems," first published between 1927 and 1930, the same period during which *Ash Wednesday* was taking shape. The "Ariel Poems" are closely related in structure, style, and meaning to those poems which eventually became sections of *Ash*

Wednesday. It is conceivable that some of the "Ariel Poems" might have been built into larger wholes and the earliest sections of *Ash Wednesday* left as separate poems. As it is, the "Ariel Poems" make a kind of series of appendixes to *Ash Wednesday*.

Turning from the external to the internal, we find in *The Hollow Men* and *Ash Wednesday* the same features already noted in earlier work. In *The Hollow Men* the themes of the fragmentary and the inarticulate are represented both by the form and the content of the statements. Throughout the poem the themes are symbolized by a wealth of images, and especially notable are "broken glass," "broken column," "broken stone," and "broken jaw." At the opening of the poem the voices of the hollow men "Are quiet and meaningless," and toward the end their speech is broken into stammered fragments of the Lord's Prayer. The first and last passages of the final section are inane and sinister parodies of a children's game song. Similar elements are present in *Ash Wednesday*. The poem begins with the translated quotation from Cavalcanti, and this is immediately broken into fragments, thus suggesting, among other things, the speaker's struggle to find expression:

> Because I do not hope to turn again
> Because I do not hope
> Because I do not hope to turn . . .

Exactly the same passage, but with "Because" changed to "Although," opens the final section of the poem. Section II is centrally concerned with fragmentation as symbolized by the scattered bones which sing, "We are glad to be scattered, we did little good to each other." As for the problem of articulation, it is the "unspoken word" which is the central concern of Section V:

> Where shall the word be found, where will the word
> Resound? Not here, there is not enough silence
> Not on the sea or on the islands, not
> On the mainland, in the desert or the rain land . . .

The final words of the poem are "Suffer me not to be separated/
And let my cry come unto Thee." These statements are fragments
quoted from Catholic ritual — and they clearly convey both of
the familiar and related themes: isolation (which is also fragmentation) and spiritual communion (which is also articulation).

In the collected editions of Eliot's poetry, placed between "Ariel
Poems" and "Minor Poems," there is a section called "Unfinished
Poems." This is comprised of *Sweeney Agonistes* and "Coriolan."
The two parts of *Sweeney Agonistes* are "Fragment of a Prologue"
and "Fragment of an Agon," and they first appeared in 1926 and
1927 respectively. Arranged together, they are described by Eliot
in a subtitle as "Fragments of an Aristophanic Melodrama." But
Sweeney Agonistes is not actually an "unfinished" work. Each part
and the two parts together are deliberate ironical parodies of surviving fragments of classical texts, and thus the fragmentariness is
a justifiable aspect of the finished product. The device of parodying
(classical) fragments provided Eliot with an opportunity for ex-
perimental exercises in the use of dramatic verse and thus also in
the use of rhythms borrowed from the conventions of the music
hall and of colloquial speech. Another aspect of the fragmentariness is the deliberate continuity with, or reiteration of, elements
from his earlier work — meaning, of course, that Sweeney had first
appeared in the quatrains of *Poems* (1920) and then again briefly in
The Waste Land. In the satirically trite and empty speech which
makes up so much of the dialogue in these pieces, the subject of
articulation, of communication, is plainly implicit, and it is finally
explicit in the lines spoken by Sweeney toward the end of the
second "Fragment":

> I gotta use words when I talk to you
> But if you understand or if you dont
> That's nothing to me and nothing to you . . .

The fragmentariness of *Sweeney Agonistes* is a structural device, but also, as in earlier works, it is related to subject and meaning. "Coriolan," on the other hand, is appropriately described as "unfinished." Its two sections, "Triumphal March" and "Difficulties of a Statesman," appeared respectively in 1931 and 1932. The work was apparently motivated by the political pressures of the time. Eliot's description of "Coriolan" as unfinished is meaningful in a number of ways. It obviously signifies that a suite of sections constituting a larger and self-contained work was intended. Eliot clearly abandoned the project at an early date, for in *Collected Poems 1909–1935* the work is already classified as unfinished. And "Coriolan" does have a quality of incompleteness in greater measure than is characteristic of Eliot's work. There is, for example, more "completeness," more clarity of effect, a more decided achievement of tone, in any section of *The Waste Land* or *The Hollow Men* or *Ash Wednesday*. Perhaps Eliot was aware of this measure of failure in deciding to abandon the project and then to classify it as unfinished. It was, in fact, uncharacteristic of Eliot to have projected a poem on so large a scale, and the failure of the project is therefore significant. When questioned by an interviewer, Eliot clearly acknowledged what was otherwise implicit in his practice. To the question as to whether *Ash Wednesday* had begun as separate poems, he answered: "Yes, like *The Hollow Men*, it originated out of separate poems. . . . Then gradually I came to see it as a sequence. That's one way in which my mind does seem to have worked throughout the years poetically — doing things separately and then seeing the possibility of fusing them together, altering them, and making a kind of whole of them."

A *kind* of whole — that is an apt and significant description. That kind of whole is nowhere more obvious than in what appears to be Eliot's final major performance in nondramatic verse, the *Four Quartets*. He has informed us that the first of these, *Burnt Norton*, grew out of passages deleted from his play *Murder in the Cathe-*

dral. The *Four Quartets* was hardly conceived as "a kind of whole" at the time of the composition of *Burnt Norton.* That poem, eventually to be the first quartet, appeared in 1935, and the next quartet, *East Coker*, not until 1940. Thus the *Four Quartets* had an unpremeditated beginning in the salvaging of fragments removed from the play. *Burnt Norton* itself becomes a "kind of fragment" in retrospect from the other quartets. In the years immediately following its appearance it received relatively little attention, while the *Four Quartets* was soon, and then often, praised as Eliot's supreme achievement. By itself, *Burnt Norton* revealed themes and elements of structure familiar enough against the background of earlier work. Like *The Waste Land*, it is divided into five sections. It has affinities of meaning and style with *Ash Wednesday* and *Murder in the Cathedral*, and also with the play *The Family Reunion*, which came later (1939). But in serving as the model for the other three quartets, it derived a clarity of structure and patterning of themes which could not otherwise be claimed for it. To extend the musical metaphor of the inclusive title, it is the variations which locate and define the theme. And it is that title which announces most succinctly the quasi-wholeness and the quasi-fragmentariness which are characteristic of Eliot's work. The title *Four Quartets* allows for the separate unity of each of the quartets, and at the same time makes each a part of the larger whole.

While this ambivalence of parts and wholes is a structural convenience of which Eliot had always availed himself, it operates with special purpose in *Four Quartets.* A central subject of the work is the relation of the individual consciousness and identity to the passage of time — and time is meaningful in the work not only as a consideration and a grounds of discourse, but also in respect to the history of the composition of *Four Quartets*, to its having been written over a period of time. During this period of time there were changes in the poet's attitudes. According to *Burnt Norton*,

"To be conscious is not to be in time." Escape from time into consciousness is achieved in the transcendant ecstasy symbolized by "the moment in the rose-garden," so that all other time, unless it is a means to this end, is meaningless:

> Ridiculous the waste sad time
> Stretching before and after.

The later quartets, on the other hand, are less subjective and are increasingly concerned with reconciling the temporal and the timeless — as toward the end of *The Dry Salvages*:

> And right action is freedom
> From past and future also.
> For most of us, this is the aim
> Never here to be realised;
> Who are only undefeated
> Because we have gone on trying . . .

Four Quartets is (or are) essentially meditative and reflective poetry, but the mode of composition over a period of time, the fresh attack in each quartet on the same themes, the willingness to acknowledge and define changes in attitude — these give a dramatic quality to the reflections. The changes wrought by time are thus not only a general subject of the work, they are a particularized and dramatized meaning, and in being such they are also a lineament of the form. The poet's awareness of this fact is among the reflections he makes in the poetry. In *East Coker* there is the plaintive observation that "every attempt / Is a wholly new start," and in *The Dry Salvages* the problem is expressed again, this time as a broader, less subjectively personal preoccupation:

> time is no healer: the patient is no longer here. . . .
> You are not the same people who left that station
> Or who will arrive at any terminus . . .

Each of the quartets and then all of them together have a greater conventional unity than Eliot's previous nondramatic poetry.

Whereas so much of the earlier work is a direct representation of the fragmentariness of experience, *Four Quartets* is a deliberate and sustained discourse on that subject, and it ends with a serene vision of that wholeness which lies beyond the reach of time:

> And all shall be well and
> All manner of thing shall be well
> When the tongues of flame are in-folded
> Into the crowned knot of fire
> And the fire and the rose are one.

As in earlier work, the problem of articulation is among the interrelated themes of *Four Quartets*. In *Ash Wednesday* blame was placed upon the external world for this problem:

> there is not enough silence . . .
> The right time and the right place are not here . . .

The same complaint is made in the early quartets, as in the final section of *Burnt Norton*:

> Words strain,
> Crack and sometimes break, under the burden,
> Under the tension, slip, slide, perish,
> Decay with imprecision, will not stay in place,
> Will not stay still. Shrieking voices
> Scolding, mocking, or merely chattering,
> Always assail them.

In *East Coker* the poet complains of "the intolerable wrestle / With words and meanings." If it is impossible to say just what he means, this is because his meanings have changed with the passage of time,

> Because one has only learnt to get the better of words
> For the thing one no longer has to say, or the
>   way in which
> One is no longer disposed to say it.

Blame is still put upon the external world, for the struggle must be made, he says, now, under conditions

That seem unpropitious.

In the final quartet, *Little Gidding*, there is greater candor, greater objectivity, an acknowledgment of his own achievement, but still a note of alienation, as the poet sees his work (so long a dominant and determining influence) recede with the passage of time into the perspective of literary history:

Last season's fruit is eaten
And the fullfed beast shall kick the empty pail.
For last year's words belong to last year's language
And next year's words await another voice.

In the last section of *Little Gidding* there is a final statement on the subject, a statement which combines a celebration of the possible with an acceptance of the inevitable.

And every phrase

And sentence that is right (where every word is at home,
Taking its place to support the others,
The word neither diffident nor ostentatious,
An easy commerce of the old and the new,
The common word exact without vulgarity,
The formal word precise but not pedantic,
The complete consort dancing together)
Every phrase and every sentence is an end and a beginning,
Every poem an epitaph.

As already noted, the isolation of the individual is a theme of Eliot's plays, and closely related to it is the problem of articulation and mutual understanding. In *The Cocktail Party*, two ways of life are set in contrast, the way of the saint and the way of ordinary experience. While it is allowed that "Both ways are necessary," that a choice must be made of one or the other, and that the ordinary way is not inferior, it is nonetheless presented unattractively. Husband and wife, representing the ordinary way, are described as

> Two people who know they do not understand each other,
> Breeding children whom they do not understand
> And who will never understand them.

If in *The Cocktail Party* there is an affirmation of the ordinary way, this affirmation includes the attitude of being resigned to isolation. With *The Confidential Clerk*, however, the polarities of absolute isolation and absolute understanding are resolved by the acceptance of intermediate possibilities, of partial understanding. Colby Simpkins, the young confidential clerk, speaks of the limitations of mutual understanding not as a negative aspect of human relations but as a ground for mutual respect:

> I meant, there's no end to understanding a person.
> All one can do is to understand them better,
> To keep up with them; so that as the other changes
> You can understand the change as soon as it happens,
> Though you couldn't have predicted it.

The Confidential Clerk ends on the theme of understanding between husband and wife and between parents and children. The aging couple, Sir Claude and Lady Elizabeth, have finally achieved a measure of understanding with each other. When she says, "Claude, we've got to try to understand our children," her illegitimate son (who is engaged to his illegitimate daughter) says — as the final words of the play — "And we should like to understand *you*." *The Elder Statesman* similarly finds dramatic resolution in the understanding achieved between the generations, between the father on the one hand and the daughter and her fiancé on the other. Toward the end of the play the familiar problem of articulation arises between the lovers, when Charles tells Monica that he loves her beyond "the limits of speech," and that the lover, despite the inadequacy of words, must still struggle for them as the asthmatic struggles for breath. Not the measure of communication achieved, but the will and effort to communicate receive the emphasis. In the dedication Eliot speaks of himself and his wife as "lovers" who share each other's thoughts "without need of speech" and who "babble . . . without need of meaning." The dedication ends with the statement that some of the words of the play have a special meaning "For you and me only." These lines document the extreme change in attitude that has taken place since Eliot first recorded Prufrock's lament that he could linger among the sea-girls of his restrained erotic fantasies only "Till human voices wake us, and we drown." In these recent lines to his wife he celebrates a mutual understanding which requires no articulation and a speech which does not strain toward meaning. In the final lines there is again the matter of words and meanings, and of isolation, but it is an isolation which is shared — "For you and me only" — and thus it is also communion — but still, in a sense, isolation. Eliot has changed his attitude without departing from his theme.

In his criticism Eliot has said a number of times that the entire output of certain writers constitutes a single work, that there is a meaningful interrelationship of compositions, and that individual pieces are endowed with meaning by other pieces and by the whole context of a writer's work. Like so many of Eliot's generalizations, this is particularly applicable to his own poetry. If there is a fragmentary aspect to much of his work, there is also a continuity and wholeness. As we have already seen, a frequent practice of Eliot's was "doing things separately" and then "making a kind of whole of them," so that the fragmentary quality of the work is finally operative in the unity of the whole. The recurrent themes of time, alienation, isolation, and articulation obviously contribute to the continuity. And so does a steadily developing pattern of interrelated images, symbols, and themes. There is for example, the underwater imagery of the poems of the "Prufrock" group:

> I should have been a pair of ragged claws
> Scuttling across the floors of silent seas.

> We have lingered in the chambers of the sea
> By sea-girls wreathed with seaweed red and brown
> Till human voices wake us, and we drown.
>
> ✔   ✔   ✔
>
> The memory throws up high and dry
> A crowd of twisted things;
> A twisted branch upon the beach . . .
>
> ✔   ✔   ✔
>
> The brown waves of fog toss up to me
> Twisted faces from the bottom of the street . . .
>
> ✔   ✔   ✔
>
> His laughter was submarine and profound
> Like the old man of the sea's
> Hidden under coral islands
> Where worried bodies of drowned men drift
>   down in the green silence,
> Dropping from fingers of surf.

Comparable images, of water and underwater, of rain and river and sea, continue to appear throughout the poetry, reflecting and echoing each other with cumulative effect. There is a similar development of flower and garden imagery, from beginning to end, and extending into the plays. The "hyacinth girl" of *The Waste Land* is related to the "smell of hyacinths" in "Portrait of a Lady," to the girl, "her arms full of flowers," in "La Figlia che Piange," and to the little girl ("Elle était toute mouillée, je lui ai donné des primevères") of "Dans le Restaurant." The rose-garden dialogue of Harry and Agatha in *The Family Reunion* remains enigmatic unless related to this garden imagery in Eliot's poetry, and especially to the symbolic rose-gardens of *Ash Wednesday* and *Burnt Norton*. Each garden passage, whether early or late, gains in clarity and scope of meaning when in relation to the others. At the outset of *The Confidential Clerk*, when Eggerson speaks of Colby —

> He's expressed such an interest in my garden
> That I think he ought to have window boxes.
> Some day he'll want a garden of his own.

— the informed reader is alerted to the spiritual and religious intimations of the ecstatic childhood experience in the rose-garden, variously represented elsewhere in Eliot's poetry. In addition to such meaningful recurrence of symbolic imagery, there is at times a merging of one kind of imagery with another, as in these lines from "Marina":

> Whispers and small laughter between leaves and hurrying feet
> Under sleep, where all the waters meet.

Here the garden imagery and the water imagery are related to each other, and related also to that deeper realm of consciousness in which such associations occur. Two patterns of imagery, each already intricate and extensive, have been joined to produce a pattern that is still larger and more intricate.

In the continuity of Eliot's poetry, there is not only an accumulation of meaning but an alteration of meaning, a retroactive effect of later elements upon earlier. For example, the lines quoted from "Marina" have a relevance to the final lines of "Prufrock." Marina is the girl, the daughter, in Shakespeare's *Pericles*, and, as her name indicates, a "sea-girl." There are, thus, in both passages the details of underwater, of sleep, and of the sea-girls. Considered alone, the sexual fantasy of the earlier passage is expressive of Prufrock's isolation and alienation — "Till human voices wake us, and we drown." But when considered in relation to "Marina" and to the entire pattern of the rose-garden imagery, Prufrock's erotic daydream becomes an intimation of what is represented in later poems as spiritual vision. The mermaids of Prufrock's self-indulgent reverie are an antecedent type of the female figure who is later to represent spiritual guidance — such as the Lady in *Ash Wednesday*, who is "spirit of the fountain, spirit of the garden . . . spirit of the river, spirit of the sea."

Another example of retroactive effect is Eliot's use of ideas found in the mystical work of St. John of the Cross, *The Dark Night of the Soul*. The Spanish mystic outlines a course of spiritual discipline leading to purgation and spiritual rebirth. The initial condition requisite for entering this discipline is described by St. John as of a negative nature, a state of inertia of sense and of spirit, the purpose being ultimately to eliminate the sensual and to bring the spiritual under control. This condition is one of isolation, alienation, bleakness, emptiness, dryness. St. John's system is summarized in *Burnt Norton* and *East Coker*, in each case in the final passage of Section III — with particular clarity in *Burnt Norton*:

> Internal darkness, deprivation
> And destitution of all property,
> Desiccation of the world of sense,
> Evacuation of the world of fancy,
> Inoperancy of the world of spirit . . .

It is this system of spiritual discipline which provides the underlying scheme of *Ash Wednesday* and which is the clue to the meaning of that poem. The renunciation and impotency of Section I, the dry and scattered bones of Section II, seem to be a reiteration of the bleaker themes of *The Waste Land* and *The Hollow Men* — but with a difference. In *Ash Wednesday* there is an acceptance of the plight, and the bones sing, "We are glad to be scattered." The wasted and hollow condition, unrelieved in the earlier poems, are in *Ash Wednesday* a preparation for "strength beyond hope and despair" (Section III). Hence the ambiguous prayer, in the first and last sections, "Teach us to care and not to care." In *Ash Wednesday* Eliot maintains the themes of the earlier poetry, but in relating them to St. John's system of spiritual discipline, the themes are reinterpreted and re-evaluated. Thus, from the perspective of *Ash Wednesday* and the *Four Quartets*, the earlier poetry takes on a meaning which it did not previously have. Once we have followed Eliot in relating his themes to St. John's system, the relevance extends to all expressions of the theme. The statement in "Gerontion," "I have lost my sight, smell, hearing, taste and touch," becomes an anticipation of "Desiccation of the world of sense." This is not to say that the earlier apparent meanings of "Gerontion," *The Waste Land*, and *The Hollow Men* are canceled out by the later poems, any more than one quartet cancels another, or the later plays the earlier plays and poems. While each work remains itself, it takes on an additional aspect, a qualification of meaning, in the larger context. Eliot's observation, in "Tradition and the Individual Talent," about literature in general, that "the past [is] altered by the present as much as the present is directed by the past," is precisely applicable to his own career as a poet.

In discussing Eliot's poetry, we have, inevitably, considered some of the ways in which the poetry and the criticism are related to each other. This intricate and extensive subject has received the attention of numerous critics, including Eliot himself in recent years. But a few more illustrations of the relation will be appropriate and will serve as a further documentation of the emphases here pursued. It is particularly some of the more famous essays which lend themselves to this purpose. For example, in "The Metaphysical Poets" (1921) we find ideas which are applicable to Eliot's poetry, such as the following familiar passage: "We can only say that it appears likely that poets in our civilization, as it exists at present, must be *difficult*. Our civilization comprehends great variety and complexity, and this variety and complexity, playing upon a refined sensibility, must produce various and complex results. The poet must become more and more comprehensive, more allusive, more indirect, in order to force, to dislocate if necessary, language into his meaning." This belongs to the period of *The Waste*

Land, and it is clearly enough an argument for such poetry. At the same time, one may see in this argument a recurring theme of Eliot's verse: the poet's struggle to state his meaning and the obstacles he faces in the contemporary world. Eliot offers the metaphysical poets as a precedent for this forcing and dislocating of language. But such deliberate struggle seems hardly to accord with the "direct sensuous apprehension of thought" and the ability to "feel their thought as immediately as the odour of a rose" which Eliot approvingly attributes to the metaphysical poets. These *direct* and *immediate* abilities of the metaphysical poets are, of course, functions of that "unified sensibility" which Eliot claimed for them. But when he speaks of them as being "engaged in the task of trying to find the verbal equivalent for states of mind and feeling," the poets would appear to be in pursuit of something rather than already in possession of it. Eliot's theory of the sensibilities — "unified and "dissociated" — which has had such tremendous influence, crumbles into confusion with his later (1931) remark that a "deep fissure" was already evident in Donne's sensibility. Whatever inconsistencies and changes there may have been in the critic's theories, it is clear that the poet's sustained preoccupation has been with "the verbal equivalent for states of mind and feeling."

This idea is repeated in the criticism in various ways and at various times throughout Eliot's career. Even the famous "objective correlative" defined in "Hamlet and His Problems" (1919) has this meaning: "The only way of expressing emotion in the form of art is by finding an 'objective correlative'; in other words, a set of objects, a situation, a chain of events which shall be the formula of that *particular* emotion; such that when the external facts, which must terminate in sensory experience, are given, the emotion is immediately evoked." Although the statement is more involved, the essential meaning is the same — the poet seeks to say exactly what he means, to find "the verbal equivalent for states of mind and feeling." Eliot's purpose in defining the objective correlative was to indicate what he considered to be a failing in Shakespeare's play: "Hamlet (the man) is dominated by an emotion which is inexpressible, because it is in *excess* of the facts as they appear. . . . We must simply admit that here Shakespeare tackled a problem which proved too much for him." It is not necessary to agree with this view of *Hamlet* in order to find it impressive – indeed, fascinating. For here again Eliot is concerned with the poet's struggle to express and evoke his meaning in all its fullness. The comment on *Hamlet* is especially interesting when compared with remarks Eliot was to make, so many years later, in the interview:

"I think that in the early poems it was a question of not being able to – of having more to say than one knew how to say, and having something one wanted to put into words and rhythm which one didn't have the command of words and rhythm to put in a way immediately apprehensible.

"That type of obscurity comes when the poet is still at the stage of learning how to use language. You have to say the thing the difficult way. The only alternative is not saying it at all, at that stage. By the time of the *Four Quartets*, I couldn't have written in the style of *The Waste Land*. In *The Waste Land*, I wasn't even bothering whether I understood what I was saying."

These remarks forcefully suggest that in the essay on *Hamlet* Eliot was characteristically preoccupied with his own problems as poet. Nor is it, again, necessary to agree with the remarks in order to find them valuable and meaningful. If Eliot's earlier meanings exceeded his ability to express them, then the inability was actually an essential part of the meanings – and the meanings were expressed, after all! For we have seen that so much of Eliot's meaning, so much of the "state of mind" evoked by his poetry, is the state of isolation, of the ineffable and inarticulate. It is impossible to conceive of Eliot's earlier meanings as having any measure of fullness without the intimations of the ineffable. We have seen how much this theme contributes to the continuity and the larger meaning of his work. Although Eliot contrasts the *Four Quartets* with *The Waste Land*, it is well to recall that in *East Coker* he says

one has only learnt to get the better of words
For the thing one no longer has to say, or the way in which
One is no longer disposed to say it.

Other comments made by the author of *The Waste Land* on his own poem serve to illustrate various aspects of his behavior as a critic. In "Thoughts after Lambeth" (1931) he said: "when I wrote a poem called *The Waste Land* some of the more approving critics said that I had expressed the 'disillusionment of a generation,' which is nonsense. I may have expressed for them their own illusion of being disillusioned, but that did not form part of my intention." This passage has been a favorite target of Eliot's detractors, but it has also been cited justly enough by more objective critics in calling attention to the haughty posturing which at times marred his pronouncements. Eliot himself was eventually to acknowledge a distaste for the pontifical tone which occasionally appears in his earlier prose. But to return to *The Waste Land* — when the interviewer observed that "more recent critics, writing after your later poetry, found *The Waste Land* Christian," Eliot answered, "No, it wasn't part of my conscious intention." We may surmise that Eliot had his own poetry in mind when in 1951 he was discussing the poetry of Virgil. He said then that while a poet may think that he has given expression to a "private experience" but "without giving himself away," his readers may find his lines expressing "their own secret feelings . . . the exultation or despair of a generation."

Much of Eliot's later criticism and comment has been concerned with readjusting his position, with recording an achieved capacity for tolerance and a catholicity of taste, and with diluting or eliminating the asperity with which he had treated various figures and issues. The essays on Tennyson, Milton, Goethe, and Kipling present such readjustments and reconsiderations. In both the prose and the poetry, Eliot has shown an increasing tendency to talk candidly about himself, and with less fear of "giving himself away." It must have been as clear to Eliot as to his readers that Harry, the protagonist of *The Family Reunion*, in his complacent suffering and arrogant isolation, was a recognizable "objective correlative" for the author — when in "Poetry and Drama" (1950), Eliot said of Harry that "my hero now strikes me as an insufferable prig." It should not be necessary to quibble about what and how much the author intended to give away in these few words. But it is well worth pondering, along with the harsh judgment of Harry, Eliot's equally sound opinion (stated in the interview) that "*The Family Reunion* is still the best of my plays in the way of poetry."

Eliot has been less concerned to publicize a readjustment of position on political and social questions than on matters of literary criticism. He has been comparatively reticent on those political pronouncements which, in the light of later history, have appeared to be in accord with Fascist programs and practices. It may at least be said for him that he was not alone in failing to envisage the brutality to which the Nazis would extend the "corrective" doctrines of the reactionary position. Closely related to some of the quasi-Fascistic pronouncements made by Eliot is the question of anti-Semitism. The distasteful portrayal of Jews in "Gerontion" and in some of the quatrains of *Poems* (1920) —

> But this or such was Bleistein's way:
> A saggy bending of the knees
> And elbows with the palms turned out,
> Chicago Semite Viennese.

— may be considered as literary grotesqueries comparable to the portraits of Sweeney and Grishkin. But the evidence of the prose is another matter. In *After Strange Gods* (1933), discussing the virtues of a regional culture and homogeneous community, he said: ". . . reasons of race and religion combine to make any large number of free-thinking Jews undesirable. . . . And a spirit of excessive tolerance is to be deprecated." The contrived allusion to Karl Marx (in 1935) as a "Jewish economist" was again an amazing lapse in dignity. Merely to assert that he was not, or is not, anti-Semitic is an insufficient reckoning with such indiscretions. But it is a well-established habit of Eliot's readers and critics to discover meanings by relating seemingly remote details from various parts of his writings. It may therefore be no excessive tolerance to apply to Eliot's earlier deprecations the splendid and moving lines, in *Little Gidding*, with which the "familiar compound ghost" describes "the gifts reserved for age":

> the conscious impotence of rage
> At human folly, and the laceration
> Of laughter at what ceases to amuse.
> And last, the rending pain of re-enactment
> Of all that you have done, and been; the shame
> Of motives late revealed, and the awareness
> Of things ill done and done to others' harm
> Which once you took for exercise of virtue.
> Then fools' approval stings, and honour stains.

In 1955 Eliot said of Wordsworth, "his name marks an epoch," and it is even more true of Eliot himself. But this has already been said in various ways by various writers with various intentions. Indeed, so much has been said about the poet, dramatist, critic of literature and culture, that any effort to add a further comment can hardly escape repetitions of the familiar. And so, to end briefly with an appropriate summation and illustration of his achievement as poet and critic, it may be most fitting to follow in the convention of quoting the man himself: ". . . the best contemporary poetry can give us a feeling of excitement and a sense of fulfilment different from any sentiment aroused by even very much greater poetry of a past age." If "next year's words await another voice," it is to be hoped that the voice will be not only different from Eliot's, but equal to it in giving us excitement and fulfillment.

⨀ Selected Bibliography

Poetry and Plays of T. S. Eliot

SEPARATE WORKS

Prufrock and Other Observations. London: The Egoist, Ltd., 1917.

Poems. Richmond (England): L. and V. Woolf, 1919.

The Waste Land. New York: Boni and Liveright, 1922; Richmond (England): L. and V. Woolf, 1923.

Ash Wednesday. London: Faber and Faber, 1930; New York: Putnam's, 1930.

Sweeney Agonistes. London: Faber and Faber, 1932.

The Rock. London: Faber and Faber, 1934.

Murder in the Cathedral. London: Faber and Faber, 1935; New York: Harcourt, Brace, 1935.

The Family Reunion. London: Faber and Faber, 1939; New York: Harcourt, Brace, 1939.

Old Possum's Book of Practical Cats. London: Faber and Faber, 1939; New York: Harcourt, Brace, 1939.

Four Quartets. New York: Harcourt, Brace, 1943; London: Faber and Faber, 1944.

The Cocktail Party. London: Faber and Faber, 1950; New York: Harcourt, Brace, 1950.

The Confidential Clerk. London: Faber and Faber, 1954; New York: Harcourt, Brace, 1954.

The Elder Statesman. London: Faber and Faber, 1959; New York: Farrar, Straus and Cudahy, 1959.

SELECTED AND COLLECTED EDITIONS

Ara Vos Prec. London: Ovid Press, 1920.

Poems. New York: Knopf, 1920.

Poems 1909–1925. London: Faber and Gwyer, 1925; New York: Harcourt, Brace, 1932.

Collected Poems 1909–1935. London: Faber and Faber, 1936; New York: Harcourt, Brace, 1936.

The Complete Poems and Plays. New York: Harcourt, Brace, 1952.

46

Prose of T. S. Eliot

SEPARATE WORKS

The Sacred Wood. London: Methuen, 1920.

Homage to John Dryden. London: L. and V. Woolf, 1924.

The Use of Poetry and the Use of Criticism. London: Faber and Faber, 1933; Cambridge, Mass.: Harvard University Press, 1933.

After Strange Gods. London: Faber and Faber, 1934; New York: Harcourt, Brace, 1934.

Elizabethan Essays. London: Faber and Faber, 1934.

The Idea of a Christian Society. London: Faber and Faber, 1939; New York: Harcourt, Brace, 1940.

Notes towards the Definition of Culture. London: Faber and Faber, 1948; New York: Harcourt, Brace, 1949.

SELECTED AND COLLECTED EDITIONS

Selected Essays 1917–1932. London: Faber and Faber, 1932; New York: Harcourt, Brace, 1932. (Enlarged editions, called *Selected Essays*, were published in New York in 1950, and in London in 1951.)

Essays Ancient and Modern. London: Faber and Faber, 1936; New York: Harcourt, Brace, 1936.

On Poetry and Poets. London: Faber and Faber, 1957; New York: Farrar, Straus and Cudahy, 1957.

Current Reprints

Christianity and Culture. New York: Harvest (Harcourt, Brace). $1.95. (This contains *The Idea of a Christian Society* and *Notes towards a Definition of Culture.*)

The Cocktail Party. London: Faber and Faber. 5s or $1.25.

Collected Poems 1909–1935. London: Faber and Faber. 5s or $1.25.

Essays on Elizabethan Drama. New York: Harvest. $1.95.

Four Quartets. London: Faber and Faber. 5s or $1.25.

The Sacred Wood. New York: Barnes and Noble. $1.25.

The Waste Land and Other Poems. New York: Harvest. $.95.

Bibliography

Gallup, Donald. *T. S. Eliot: A Bibliography.* London: Faber and Faber, 1952; New York: Harcourt, Brace, 1953. (Besides listing all editions of Eliot's books and pamphlets through 1951, this includes books and pamphlets edited or with contributions by Eliot, his contributions to periodicals, translations of his writings into foreign languages, and recordings of his readings. Earlier versions of this book were *A Catalogue of English and American First Editions of the Writings of T. S. Eliot*, 1937, and *A Bibliographical Check-list of the Writings of T. S. Eliot*, 1947, both published in New Haven by the Yale University Library.)

Interpretive and Critical Studies

Braybrooke, Neville, ed. *T. S. Eliot: A Symposium for His Seventieth Birthday*. London: Hart-Davis, 1958.

Drew, Elizabeth. *T. S. Eliot: The Design of His Poetry*. New York: Scribner's, 1949.

Gardner, Helen. *The Art of T. S. Eliot*. London: Cresset Press, 1949; New York: Dutton, 1959 (paperback).

Green, E. J. H. *T. S. Eliot et la France*. Paris: Boivin, 1951.

Jones, David E. *The Plays of T. S. Eliot*. London: Routledge and Kegan Paul, 1960.

Kenner, Hugh. *The Invisible Poet: T. S. Eliot*. New York: McDowell, Obolensky, 1959.

March, Richard, and Tambimuttu, eds. *T. S. Eliot: A Symposium*. London: Editions Poetry, 1948; Chicago: Regnery, 1949.

Matthiessen, F. O. *The Achievement of T. S. Eliot*. New York: Oxford, 1935. Second edition. enlarged, 1947. Third edition, with additional chapter by C. L. Barber, 1958. Paperback, 1959.

Maxwell, D. E. S. *The Poetry of T. S. Eliot*. London: Routledge and Kegan Paul, 1952.

Preston, Raymond. *Four Quartets Rehearsed*. New York: Sheed and Ward, 1946.

Rajan, B., ed. *T. S. Eliot: A Study of His Writings by Several Hands*. London: Dobson, 1947.

Robbins, R. H. *The T. S. Eliot Myth*. New York: Schuman, 1951.

Smidt, Kristian. *Poetry and Belief in the Work of T. S. Eliot*. Oslo: Jacob Dybwad, 1949.

Smith, Grover. *T. S. Eliot's Poetry and Plays: A Study in Sources and Meaning*. Chicago: University of Chicago Press, 1956. The third impression, 1960, is enlarged, paperback.

Unger, Leonard, ed. *T. S. Eliot: A Selected Critique*. New York: Rinehart, 1948.

Williamson, George. *A Reader's Guide to T. S. Eliot*. New York: Noonday Press, 1953. Paperback, 1957.